It's All In Your Mind

By James Bars

This book is a summary or
Chapter One of our book ~

*The Nourished Soul ~ Nurturing Your Mind to
Grow Unending Health and Happiness*

Published by Home Of Love Publications

Editor: Blake Bars

Cover Image: Fotilia

Cover Design: James Bars

ISBN: 978-0-9970183-9-4

"Come to me, all you who are weary and burdened, and I will give you rest. Take my yoke upon you and learn from me, for I am gentle and humble in heart, and you will find rest for your souls." Matthew 11:28-29 NIV

It's All In Your Mind

"If you can change your mind, you can change your life." — William James

"More than anything you guard, protect your mind, for life flows from it." Proverbs 4:23 CEB

The incomprehensible powers and abilities of your brain are without equal among earth's other organisms. Your mind is your brain in action. Physically, you are a combination of earth, water and that elusive yet ever-present power of God, known as the breath of life. Spiritually, you are a force for good or evil. Whoever you become here and hereafter will be determined by the choices you make with your mind.

Your extraordinary brain is a mere three-pound (1.4 kilograms) mass of jelly-like fats and tissues, yet it's the most complex of all known living structures. It comprises less than three percent of your body's weight but uses 20 percent of your body's energy. [E] Your extraordinary brain decidedly sets you apart from all other earthly creatures. [F]

Your brain holds approximately 1.25 terabytes of data and performs at around 100 teraflops (one hundred trillion point operations per second).

No computer built by man can do what your brain can do. Designed and built by God, your brain can choose to move its body from place to place. A computer cannot. Your brain can experience emotions, rewire

4

itself based on new experiences or changes in understanding, and even grow new components (neurons). A computer cannot. Ultimately, your brain is the most marvelous, sophisticated, biological piece of engineering known, far beyond human ingenuity and immeasurably more complex than anything built by man.

Your ability to love and care, is primarily located in the front portion of your brain and referred to as your prefrontal cortex. This area processes most of your conscious decisions and produces nearly all of your love-based emotions. [A] This is the part of your brain where wisdom and understanding create sound judgment, and your soul is either blessed, or you experience the unhealthy consequences of veering from God's laws of love and liberty. It is in the prefrontal cortex that the proverbial heart and soul of a person appear to be located and where your free-choice decisions are made.

If you seek them, God's soul-enriching assets of wisdom, knowledge, discretion, and understanding will be planted in your mind to preserve you and deliver you from the ravages of evil. *"When wisdom enters your heart, and knowledge is pleasant to your soul, discretion will preserve you; understanding will keep you, to deliver you from the way of evil."* Proverbs 2:10-12 NKJV

It is interesting to note that the mark of the beast as well as the seal of God, mentioned in the book of Revelation, both occur in the forehead where your prefrontal cortex is located. Your free-choice decisions are built in this area of your brain. Choose well, my friend. Be wise.

God created your brain to coordinate all of your physical actions and mental processes and to function as a communication device. Through your brain, you are enabled to communicate with other beings and commune with the Creator of the Universe—directly. Fascinating, isn't it?

Your **M**otives, **A**ffections, **D**esires, **F**eelings, **A**ctions, and **T**houghts (Your *MADFATs*—to be discussed at length throughout this book) are rooted in your brain through neural pathways.

Many of your neural pathways were inherited; many more were created the first time you thought something, felt something, sensed something, tasted something, heard something, touched something, saw something, or smelled something—actually, anytime you experienced anything.

As an experience occurs, a thin neural fiber is physically created in your brain. If you looked at your brain under a high-powered microscope, you could see these fibers. There are hundreds of millions of them. [H]

5

These neural pathways are in a state of continual flux. Some will stay, and some will go. Every time you re-experience the same event that particular neural pathway is reinforced and more likely to be retained as a character trait, belief, or choice pattern. [A]

Planting and nurturing neural pathways that promote thriving health and happiness can be compared with how raindrops produce rivers. The more raindrops that seep into a pathway, the easier it is for subsequent raindrops to travel down that same pathway. This is how rivers are formed, and it is the way many of your *MADFATs*, habitual behaviors, and beliefs are developed—through repeated use of the same pathways.

You assign pleasure or pain to each experience and either seek it again if you believe it is pleasurable or avoid it if you believe it is painful. Nearly all your behaviors are based on and controlled by these two simple yet powerful desires:

1) The desire to avoid discomfort and pain.
2) The desire to obtain happiness and pleasure.

With each new experience and each new neural pathway created in your brain, you may create a river of habit if you decide it is pleasurable. However, if you decide the experience is too painful, either immediately or if you can see that it will create too much pain in the long run, that trickle or river (neural pathway) will dry up and be eliminated from your habitual life patterns. As you follow God into the light, your *MADFATs* change, which causes physical changes in your brain. God created you to experience security, health, happiness, love, joy, peace, and pleasure when you live in harmony with His original design. [A]

The brain God gave you releases chemicals through neural pleasure circuits that enable you to feel good when participating in thought patterns and behaviors necessary to live, enjoy life, and procreate. A few familiar joy-givers include; romance, love, marriage, sex, family, nutrition, exercise, prayer, meditation, charitable endeavors, sunny days, cheerful people, and relaxation. Daring adventures into superior lifestyle choices will elevate joyous delights within you and flow peacefully to the world around you. Invest time and energy often in these types of activities, and both your brain and your body will reward you with happy, healthy days.

The inspiring chemicals these activities release in your brain are known as neurotransmitters and are beneficial for your physical heart as well as your spiritual heart.

Your (spiritual heart) encompasses your beliefs and worldviews,

6

including your (*MADFATs*) motives, affections, desires, feelings, actions, and thoughts. It has much to do with determining your well-being. Your spiritual heart is often the guide who chooses your mental and physical activities. When your spiritual heart is healthy and happy, your physical heart is more likely to experience the same conditions.

Your spiritual heart weighs and selects competing thought patterns and behaviors. The subsequent payoffs they produce will determine your states of being through the release of neurotransmitters and hormones. Two of the most potent and necessary neurotransmitters are serotonin and dopamine. These two neurotransmitters are responsible for most of your feelings of wellness, inner peace, and happiness.

Good *MADFATs* often release pleasurable neurotransmitters. Bad *MADFATs* often release stress hormones that involve the brain's fight or flight systems, such as adrenaline, cortisol, and norepinephrine. These stress hormones, if overused, can be destructive and deadly.

Inner peace enhances your life. Excessive stress damages your brain and body.

Research indicates that the average person experiences somewhere between 12,000 and 60,000 thoughts per day, most of which are a repeat of standard habitual thoughts. [K]

The sad news is that the majority of your habitual thoughts are negative! This condition affects nearly every human on the planet and is known as the negativity bias. The negativity bias is a human propensity to prefer to assimilate and dwell upon negative experiences over positive or neutral ones, even if the negative experiences have little relevance. This tendency leaves us feeling the burn of being scolded more intensely than the delight of being celebrated.

Planet earth can be a dangerous place. You likely discovered this long before you were out of diapers. Your brain began building danger warning neural pathways at a very early age. These danger warning neural pathways and the fight or flight components in your brain's onboard warning systems are activated early and often. So it seems natural for you to develop dominant neural pathways that focus on avoiding danger, thus generating a negativity bias.

You may also delegate space and time to worry about negative experiences others may have, particularly those you love and care for, especially your children and theirs.

People worry. It may be a symptom of the negativity bias humans contend with in this challenging world. Since the Covid—19 pandemic began viciously attacking our planet, two widely spread words have now become nearly as common as a goodbye. Those words are—stay safe.

What do you think occurs in this cycle once you have children. That's right. The volume often increases dramatically cause now you have even more to worry about.

Life is full of positive as well as negative experiences. You record both and often award the negative one's greater worth as you navigate the rough edges of your earthly existence. Negative thoughts can get more exercise than positive thoughts because they are often repeated repeatedly until they have firmly claimed large amounts of mental real estate.

This habit of repeating the same negative thoughts day after day may be one of the primary reasons why legal and illegal mind/mood-altering drugs are so popular. People often suffer from continually watching for danger and from the relentless stress generated by the negativity bias. Their brains may get battle-weary and so low on beneficial neurotransmitters that they can't seem to feel happy, healthy, or even well.

According to the Center for Disease Control and Prevention (CDC), nearly 13% of the world's population was taking anti-depressants between 2015 and 2018. I'll bet the fallout from Covid-19 and other recent life-on-planet-earth challenges have increased that number substantially. [L]

While there are people who do suffer from clinical depression, others may simply be down in the dumps as a result of negative thinking and the actions that follow. If you struggle with depression, medication may help. You should seek professional assistance. Be prayerful and careful. God instructs us to guard and protect our minds. Remember: *"More than anything you guard, protect your mind, for life flows from it."* Proverbs 4:23 CEB

Whether you take medications or not, positive thinking and lifestyle choices are highly likely to help. Solomon was right when he wrote, *"A cheerful look brings joy to the heart, and good news health to the bones."* Proverbs 15:30 NIV

With this thought in mind, you may wish to consider avoiding the prevailing winds of negativity blown into your mind from sources such as the news, gossip, and the media. A large percentage of all mental and physical illnesses are often generated or worsened by a person's own bleak thoughts and perspectives. [B]

The good news—it is possible to rewire the habit patterns of your brain. The Apostle Paul's directive concerning our restoration process will genuinely become increasingly realized in your life. He wrote: *"Do not conform to the pattern of this world, but be transformed by the renewing of your mind. Then you will be able to test and approve what God's will is—his good, pleasing and perfect will."* Romans 12:2 NIV

Place your soul in God's care and allow His Spirit to guide you in the rewiring of your *MADFATs*. Participating in this cream-of-the-crop process will facilitate the transcendent renewing of your mind and progressively transform you into a enriched gold mine of happiness and health.

Being transformed by the renewing of your mind is a concept you will consistently encounter throughout this book. You will also occasionally uncover replays of a variety of pertinent thoughts, Scripture verses, and phrases. This is intentional. This has been done as a means of assisting in the process of planting, reinforcing, and solidifying vital neural pathways in your mind. You will perform your newly enlightened spiritual skills at a higher level as you practice them.

You are good at many things. A few of your talents were granted at birth. However, many of the skills you perform well require continual practice. Even the skills you have naturally will fade if unused. This is also intentional. God designed your brain. It has features you may not be aware of. Your brain is designed to dissolve patterns you don't use and reinforce and sustain those you do. God engineered your brain to be re-programmable. It will displace old patterns as new ones are given priority. Your brain is the most fascinating, complex, and powerful man-operated device on the planet.

A study by the National Institutes of Health reveals that negative thoughts stimulate the area of the brain where depression, fear, and anxiety arise—the right prefrontal cortex. Conversely, positive, uplifting, and joyful thoughts take place in the left prefrontal cortex. [M]

You can consciously regulate whether your right or left prefrontal cortex is stimulated by how you focus your thoughts. As your thought patterns change, the physical structure of your brain changes. This is because of brain neuroplasticity, which is its ability to be rewired. Your brain continues to adapt and change throughout your lifetime. So the old saying, *"You can't teach an old dog new tricks,"* is not true regarding your brain.

You can learn to be healthy and happy in the same way you learn to play a musical instrument—through practice. Your brain and daily life can and will change as you practice and focus your thoughts on positive, God-inspired inclinations.

Your brain is the distributor of the happy drugs—dopamine and serotonin. [N] These drugs are natural anti-depressants. You can help enable your brain to release these happy drugs through exercising positive, uplifting thoughts, physical exercise, eating healthy, nourishing foods, drinking plenty of pure water, spending time out in the clean, fresh air and sunshine, getting enough sleep, as well as other positive lifestyle choices.

Serotonin and dopamine levels are reduced as a result of stress, sleep loss, lack of exposure to sunlight, poor nutrition, and lack of exercise. Low levels of serotonin and dopamine can be the source of issues such as restlessness, tiredness, irritability, obsessive compulsions, weight gain, anxiety, chronic body pains, depression, and aggressiveness.

Lifestyle choices do affect your life. God designed you for optimal functioning when you properly maintain your systems as a whole and observe His laws of life, love, and health.

You may have made some negative life choices—you are human. Don't be discouraged by your past or current failures. You will come to view them as some of your greatest assets. Few souls are transformed instantly. Your heart's restoration will take time, effort, and practice. Enjoy the journey—delight in your successes and view failures not as losses but as opportunities to learn.

In pursuing any worthy endeavor—vision, sincere effort, and diligent practice are essential. Just like learning a musical instrument, mind renewal will take commitment and practice.

Anything you visualize as real, and repeatedly practice, is more likely to become a natural and automatic part of your daily life as those specific neural pathways are reinforced. [Q] Studies reveal this to be especially true when you meditate, pray, visualize and engage in contemplative activities.

An investigation by the Institute of Noetic Research revealed that meditation and other forms of mindful concentration strengthen and improve function in two critical brain areas—the prefrontal cortex and the insula. These improvements produced increased abilities in attention to one's own interior condition as well as enhanced empathy toward others. [R]

As you meditate on God and His word, practice His loving, peace-filled presence, visualize the uplifting realities of Him, and engage in contemplative, other-focused activities, your brain becomes physically altered. Purposely focusing your mind on the incredible truths and blessing granted by God elevates your thoughts and ennobles both your interior and public lives. Positive, uplifting, Spirit-inspired neural pathways are created and reinforced. You become better able to track the internal state of your being as well as the feelings of other people. Your level of empathy increases and your life's core motivations shift.

Your preferences are brought into alignment with God's will for you. You become spiritually, mentally, and physically transformed. This happens by God's design. He created your brain with the capacity to improve—limitlessly.

Neuroplasticity, your brain's fascinating mechanism for constant restructuring, can refer to changes in neural pathways and synapses due to changes in beliefs, behavior, environment, and ways of thinking.

Seeking and following the advice and guidance of God will help renew the physical connections in your brain. Allow Him to demonstrate and teach you His *MADFATs,* and they may become your *MADFATs.* Through this process, your mind, purposes, appetites, and passions will flow into the path of restoration. You become reborn. The old will go—the new will come. You will be transformed by the renewing of your mind. Negativity, self-centeredness, rebellion, and fear are diminished as they are replaced with God-centeredness, other-centeredness, caring, and love.

This book regularly addresses the devastating repercussions of negativity, self-centeredness, rebellion, and fear that often attend poor-choices. As God restores you, these dark aspects will slip away.

Unhealthy stress hormones often flood the brain when it is negatively or fearfully focused on the past or the future. In these places, you can get into trouble. Don't do that. *Be Here Now!*

Each moment contains elements of good and evil. You decide which will compose your thoughts.

Most moments of life are perfect opportunities to rejoice. Why not enjoy each educational moment rather than torment yourself with disturbing thoughts about the past and the future?

God exists in the present. Breathe deep these words: *Be here now!* It is a peaceful place.

Have you ever taken a drive on a beautiful day through some gorgeous scenery and not even noticed it because you were lost in your head worrying about something? Do you know why?

It is likely due to the system of neural pathways and circuits that populate your brain. Often these include a storehouse of resentments over harms done (real or imagined), regrets over issues from the past, or fears over issues that may or may not occur in the future. These are frequent repeats of the resentments, regrets, and fears that you resented, regretted, and feared the day before, and the day before that, and the day before that—you get the picture.

Your brain may be trained to focus on negative, fearful, worrisome thoughts. The more you use these neural circuits, the stronger they

11

become, and the more often you experience the resentments, regrets, fears, and worries associated with them. You go where you focus. Where is your focus? What is the fruit of a negatively focused brain? Fear!

Fear and its devastating fallout upon your heart, mind, soul, and body will diminish your ability to love, grow, develop, and experience healthy thinking. Fear, and its ruinous, self-centered manifestations of pride, greed, anger, lust, envy, gluttony, and sloth, will reduce your potential as a child of God. Fear ignites your alarm center and increases insecurity, selfishness, rage, jealousy, envy, and aggression. [A]

Love and its flourishing, God-centered and other-centered manifestations of joy, peace, patience, kindness, goodness, faithfulness, gentleness, and self-control will envelop your heart, when practiced, and leave you pleasantly fulfilled and content. Healthy love relaxes your limbic system, counters the effects of fear, and assists you in the expansion of positive, uplifting abilities.

As you free love—love will free you. Developing tangible, well-practiced, alternative neural pathways of love and care will override your inherited and cultivated neural pathways of fear and selfishness, and you will begin to enjoy life like never before. When you leave unhealthy, self-centered neural circuits idle, your brain trims them back. [A]

God has given you His Spirit of ingenious power and a talented mind that *can* be made increasingly wise and robustly new. His laws of love *can* be written on your heart. You *can* increase your levels of happiness and health. God and you together *can* rewire your *MADFATs!* Your brain *can* be renewed because of the God-designed process known as neurogenesis.

Early discoveries in the process of neurogenesis (birth of neurons in the brain) began during research in songbirds. The Society for Neuroscience developed theories concerning the ability of the human brain to participate in the process of neurogenesis by studying the ability of songbirds to learn new songs. They upheld the theory that humans do generate new neurons, but these new neurons don't survive for very long if they aren't put into use by connecting with other neurons. [V]

Neuroscience has shown that the most active area of neurogenesis is the hippocampus, a region deep within the brain involved in learning and memory. The multitude of new cells released by the hippocampus each day must be put to work in order to survive and thrive. If they don't connect, they wither and die. [W] An inspiring way to put new neurons to work is to actively seek out and focus on positive, uplifting thoughts and activities. This will help enable you to rise above the negativity bias that most humans must contend with.

Neurogenesis involves neuroplasticity, which, in part, is the idea that as your thoughts change, the physical connections in your brain change. [x]

The practice of any thought or action connects neurons and ensures their survival. Refraining from any thought or action deprives neurons of connection and ensures their death. You become what you think about, and what you think about is what you feed your heart, mind, and soul.

One purpose of this book is to provide a means to help feed your heart, mind, and soul a consistent gourmet feast at the banquet table of God. Delightful delicacies of forever fruit—yum! *"Taste and see that the Lord is good; blessed is the one who takes refuge in him."* Psalm 34:8 NIV

As you partake of the sweet fruit of His Spirit, God satisfies the deepest hunger of your soul.

You will more readily plant new neural pathways in your brain through visualizing, meditating on, writing, and practicing the use of them. As you consistently meditate on the truths God reveals to you, visualize them as your reality, record them on paper and embody them repeatedly in thought and action, new neural circuits will connect in your brain and survive. This is the process by which your *MADFATs* are rewired. God and you together will displace the darkness by filling your heart, mind, and soul with an abundance of light-bearing truth. This is an automatic process because of the way God designed your brain to be re-programmable. He knew you would need this ability when He created Adam and Eve.

God knows the end from the beginning. Since the foundation of the world, He prepared a plan for your redemption and renewal. God has given you everything you need for life and godliness. This includes a heart that can be restored, your beautiful, re-programmable brain, and the unending power He gives you through His Holy Spirit.

Ralph Waldo Emerson encapsulates the importance of allowing God to renew your thinking patterns in his famous quote: *"Sow a thought, and you reap an action; sow an action, and you reap a habit; sow a habit, and you reap a character; sow a character, and you reap a destiny."* [AAA]

As God's Spirit inspires, enables, and empowers you to assist Him in rewiring your motives, affections, desires, feelings, actions, and thoughts, the physical connections in your brain are renewed. The result will be ever-expanding—purity in your character, happiness in your days and, overall health in your life.

These are the natural results of following Him and His directions. The path of purity, happiness, and health is often a bumpy one—but it is the most rewarding journey of your earthly life and the challenge of this spiritual quest.

"How can a young person stay on the path of purity? By living according to your word. I seek you with all my heart; do not let me stray from your commands. I have hidden your word in my heart that I might not sin against you. Praise be to you, LORD; teach me your decrees."
Psalm 119:9-12 NIV

Through planting, meditating on, visualizing, and storing God's guidance in your heart, self-centeredness is diminished, rebellion is dissolved, fear is replaced with love, and the path of purity, health, and happiness is cleared.

The *Nourished Soul's Eden Treats Sheets* (located in the back half of our book entitled: *The Nourished Soul ~ Nurturing Your Mind to Grow Unending Health and Happiness*) were designed to provide a place to practice and focus on allowing God's Spirit to build, restore and reinforce valuable, new neural pathways that can enable you to walk according to the vital wisdom He has revealed. It is by consistently exposing yourself to and walking in God's love and light that you become enlightened, and your heart, mind, and soul are restored.

The act of visualizing and recording events in writing holds particular interest. It seems that visualizing and writing affect the brain's ability to retain information in unique ways.

Writing something down while considering the concepts behind the content creates a phenomenon in the brain that makes it believe the event is real. This is similar to the experience that occurs when you visualize performing a skill at a higher level—you often improve. [T]

Writing things down enhances the brain's ability to store them, especially if the message is emotionally-generated. Experiences are retained in your brain more readily and solidly if they occur in an emotional context. It seems that most decisions are charged with emotion. When you're happy and healthy, you are in a better emotional state and are more likely to make sound decisions.

It is common knowledge that those who have specific written goals are more likely to achieve them. These are the reasons why daily completing the *Nourished Soul's Eden Treats Sheets* is so vital to your regeneration process. While completing your *Nourished Soul's Eden Treats Sheets*, and throughout each day, you will record, meditate on, visualize, and embody God's transformation of your being. During this process, it is critical that you see God clearly. Your insight into His love-based character and movements is fundamental to who you will become.

As you move through the pages of this book, you will hopefully get a clear portrait of who God is. God has three towering characteristics that define His essence: (1) God is love. (2) God is light, and (3) there is no darkness in him at all. ^{1 John 4:8 NLT & 1 John 1:5 NLT}

There is a lot of misinformation about God's character. I believe He longs to lift you above any misconceptions you may have about Him and how He is dealing with the rebellion we are all born into. Scripture reveals that a personal, knowing relationship with God is the Way to eternal life. Jesus explains: *"Now this is eternal life: that they know you, the only true God, and Jesus Christ, whom you have sent."* ^{John 17:3 NIV}

Revelations concerning God's character and the depth of His love for you will unfold as you travel this trail. May you know Him well.

Rebellious self-centeredness and fear are the core patterns of life in our world. Scripture declares:

"Do not conform to the pattern of this world, but be transformed by the renewing of your mind. Then you will be able to test and approve what God's will is—his good, pleasing and perfect will." ^{Romans 12:2 NIV}

The preceding verse's instructions are achieved more easily when you see God as He truly is—love and light. If your perception of God is fear-based, this style of thinking may cause damage to your brain. You will find a clear case for love-based living by observing the example set by Jesus Christ, Who demonstrated God's true character. He did this by walking in, living in, and directing you to follow Him in—love and light. In following Him, your focus can shift from fear to love, from sickness to health, and from depression to happiness!

God will build the *New You* atop a foundation of love; if you approve. He will not force Himself upon you at any time. He cherishes your freedom of choice. You will be the deciding factor. Your cooperation is paramount to His success in renewing you. You decide whether to follow Him or not.

You decide which neural circuits get fed and survive. You decide whether your brain is full of positive or negative thought and belief patterns. Strive to keep your motives, affections, desires, feelings, actions, and thoughts focused on instilling God's positive, uplifting, and boundless qualities of love and caring. As a result, health and happiness will ripen like a bowl of sweet, refreshing, succulent goodness—Yummy!

God's love for you is as real as the ground you stand on. His desires for you to know Him well and enjoy the satisfying fruits of an intimate and caring relationship with Him rain profusely from the hearts of Him and His. In Him reside complete joy and able health.

Through the acts of visualizing, practicing, meditating on, and recording events in writing regularly, the delights revealed in this book will assist you in focusing your mental energies on crucial areas of God's will for your spiritual, mental, and physical health and happiness.

When you utilize and reinforce positive, God-focused, and other-focused neural pathways, these are strengthened, and your interior and public lives are healed. Your very presence becomes a joyful experience where God, you, and others are honored.

Alternatively, when you utilize and reinforce negative, fear-based, self-centered neural pathways, these are strengthened, and your interior and public lives are robbed of the best God hopes for you. Your world becomes a dark place where God, you, and those whose lives you touch struggle and often clash. This is the turbulence that rumbles between the dark one as he attempts to rule over this world, and God's kingdom of love and light as it draws you away from the dark side.

You are the determining variable in the skirmish over your soul.

An ancient Native American legend illustrates the conflict that may arise in you as you seek the path of health, happiness, purity and honor. The tale goes something like this:

A young warrior found himself struggling with uncontrollable urges and unhealthy desires. He went to the spiritual leader of his Tribe and explained his troubles. He wanted to live a happy, healthy, pure, and honorable life, but he continued to lose the battle against his character defects.

The elder drew him into a lush meadow where they could be with the Creator. He asked him to sit, close his eyes and breathe in the sweet, loving presence of the One Who knows all.

The young warrior relaxed and drifted readily into a state of transcendence as he connected his soul with the Spirit of God. Love and light filled the corners of his being with peace. Acceptance enveloped his troubled heart and washed away his isolation.

As he drank in the consuming flood of love and care emanating from the Creator's heart, the elder spoke softly. "You have two wolves inside of you. A white wolf and a dark wolf—they are striving for your allegiance. One will be victorious over the other."

The elder then rose quietly and drifted into the woods toward a stream. As he knelt, he cupped his hands, filled them with refreshing, pure water, and began to drink. The warrior appeared silently beside him. The elder knew his thoughts but said nothing.

After a moment, the warrior asked. "Which one wins?"

The elder took another drink, sat beside the stream in the soft grass, raised his face toward the warm, summer sun, and said. "That's easy, my son—the one you feed."

Which one will you feed? Whose warrior are you? Solomon wrote: *"Whoever seeks good finds favor, but evil comes to one who searches for it."* Proverbs 11:27 NIV

It is within the heart, mind, and soul of a person that destiny is determined. This is why Jesus instructs you to: *"Love the Lord your God with all your heart and with all your soul and with all your mind and with all your strength."* Mark 12:30 NIV

Love-based living is a parent of health and happiness and a pathway to a peaceful, free spirit.

Even though you were born broken, you can be renewed, rewired, and eternally restored. However, you have a serious dilemma—you lack the appropriate power.

To rewire your brain correctly, you will want to continually access and receive the indwelling presence of God's Holy Spirit. It is His Spirit Who bestows upon you vital, life-changing power! Feed your heart at the table of His unending feast of love and light, and your spirit will be contentedly refreshed.

Your heart, mind, and soul hunger for vital nutrients to be fed regularly into your love-based neural circuits. As you continue to apply your focus to whatever is healthy, happy, true, noble, and right, your brain will automatically begin to vanquish the dark wolf's negative patterns.

If fed a clean diet of only healthy programming, your brain will dissolve unused, negative neural circuits and nourish, enrich and secure the neural circuits that ensure victory for the white wolf within you. Your health is affected by what you eat—spiritually, mentally, and physically. Eat well, my freind. When you do, your soul will soar high above the grey, acrid stench of sickness, sadness, and the darkness that seeks to annihilate your secured, heavenly future. Instead, your healthy, happy heart will overflow with love, joy, peace, and patience.

You will be transformed by the renewing of your mind. Your time here on earth and your eternal destiny will brighten. You are not here by mistake. You are here by design. The architect of life created all and upholds all—including you. God is the Source of all life, power, wisdom, knowledge, and understanding. Perhaps the single most valuable truth a human soul may come to know is contained in the following verses. It is written:

The Son is the image of the invisible God, the firstborn over all

creation. *For in him all things were created: things in heaven and on earth, visible and invisible, whether thrones or powers or rulers or authorities; all things have been created through him and for him. He is before all things, and in him all things hold together. And he is the head of the body, the church; he is the beginning and the firstborn from among the dead, so that in everything he might have the supremacy. For God was pleased to have all his fullness dwell in him, and through him to reconcile to himself all things, whether things on earth or things in heaven, by making peace through his blood, shed on the cross.*

Once you were alienated from God and were enemies in your minds because of your evil behavior. But now he has reconciled you by Christ's physical body through death to present you holy in his sight, without blemish and free from accusation—if you continue in your faith, established and firm, and do not move from the hope held out in the gospel.

This is the gospel that you heard and that has been proclaimed to every creature under heaven, and of which I, Paul, have become a servant. Colossians 1:15-23 NIV

May God grant you an abundance of wisdom, willingness, and spiritual power as together, you transform your life through the heavenly art of mind renewal. May, His most relevant promise, delivered through Isaiah, become your reality: *"You will keep in perfect peace all who trust in you, all whose thoughts are fixed on you!"* Isaiah 26:3 NLT

If you found this booklet helpful, we would greatly appreciate it if you would bless our work with a quick review at Amazon.com. Thank you.

If you would like to elavate your growth, you may own the full version of this journey through our website, *ExploringGodsLove.com,* and *Amazon.com* under the title: *The Nourished Soul ~ Nurturing Your Mind to Grow Unending Health and Happiness.*

I am very grateful for any opportunity I get to share my gracious and wonder-filled Papa God with others. Thank you for spending a bit of your time with me. I hope to meet you one day, whether here or in eternity. I pray for God's rich blessings upon you and yours. Until then, my prayer for you and yours will be:

The Lord bless you and keep you; the Lord make his face shine on you and be gracious to you; the Lord turn his face toward you and give you peace. Numbers 6:24-26 NIV

Love, peace, and joy—in Him,
James Bars

Resources—Access books on our website's resources page at _ExploringGodsLove.com_

A. Jennings, Timothy R. M.D. The God-Shaped Brain, InterVarsity Press 2013.

E. . . . .
Swaminathan, Nikhil. Scientific American, Why Does the Brain Need So Much Power? April 29, 2008, http://www.scientificamerican.com/article.cfm?id=why-does-the-brain-need-stimulus

F. . . . .
Bartz, Paul A. We Are Fearfully and Wonderfully Made! Christian Assemblies International, http://www.cai.org/bible-studies/we-are-fearfully-and-wonderfully-made

G. Wikipedia, Brain, 18 March 2012, http://en.wikipedia.org/wiki/Brain

H. . . . .
The Kavli Foundation. Frontiers in Neuroscience, June 2007, http://www.kavli-foundation.org/frontiers-neuroscience

I. . . . .
Jennings, Timothy R. Does Conversion Heal the Brain?, September, 3 2010, http://www.comeandreason.com/index.php?option=com_content&view=article&id=309:addictions-does-conversion-heal-the-brain&catid=52:tims-blog-archive&Itemid=70

J. . . . .
Universe Review. Nerves and Nervous System, http://universe-review.ca/R10-16-ANS.htm

K. . . . .
Hawthorne, Jennifer Read. Change Your Thoughts, Change Your World, 2009, http://www.jenniferhawthorne.com/articles/change_your_thoughts.html

L. . . . .
Wehrwein, Peter. Harvard Health Letter: Astounding Increase In Antidepressant Use By Americans, October 20 2011, http://www.health.harvard.edu/blog/astounding-increase-in-antidepressant-use-by-americans-201110203624

M. . . . .
National Institute of Mental Health, The National Institute of Mental Health

Strategic Plan, 2007, http://www. nimh.nih.gov/about/strategic-planning-re-ports/index.shtml

N...

Hansen, Dirk. Neuroaddiction: The Reward Pathway, 2010, http://dirkhanson.org/neuroaddiction.html

O. Farrenkopf, Christine. Cocaine and the Brain: The Neurobiology of Addiction, 1/4/2008,...
....
http://serendip.brynmawr.edu/exchange/node/1704

P. Nestler, Eric J. and Malenka, Robert C. Scientific American, The Addicted Brain, March ....
....
2004, http://wireheading.com/article/addiction.html

Q. NeuroRehabilitation & Neuropsychological Services, P.C. The Brain and Its Functions, ...
....
http://thebrainlabs.com/brain.shtml

R. Hansen, Rick. Self-Directed Neuroplasticity: A 21st-Century View of Medita-tion, April ....
....
2011, http://www.noetic.org/noetic/issue-nine-april/self-directed-neuroplasti-city/

S. ....
Newburg, Andrew M.D. How God Changes Your Brain: Breakthrough Findings from a Leading Neuroscientist, Ballantine Books 2009

T. ....
Wax, Dustin M. Writing and Remembering: Why We Remember What We Write, September, 2011, http://www.lifehack.org/articles/productivity/writing-and-remembering- ....
why-we-remember-what-we-write.html Don't Be Stupid: A Guide To Learning, Studying, And Succeeding At College, Creative Commons, 2008

AAA. Emerson, Ralph Waldo, Goodreads—Quotable Quotes, http://www.goodreads.com/quotes/416934-sow-a-thought-and-you-reap-an-action-sow-an

James Bars Books and Booklets

Please visit our website *ExploringGodsLove.com* to access other books and booklets.

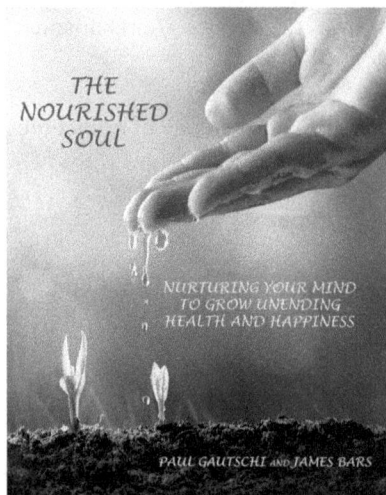

The Nourished Soul ~ Nurturing Your Mind to Grow Unending Health and Happiness

"More than anything you guard, protect your mind, for life flows from it."
Proverbs 4:23 CEB

The incomprehensible powers and abilities of your brain are without equal among earth's other organisms. Your mind is your brain in action. Whoever you become here and hereafter will be determined by the choices you make with your mind. Love or fear will dominate your thought life. You decide which one gets fed.

Love and its flourishing manifestations of joy, peace, patience, kindness, goodness, faithfulness, gentleness, and self-control will envelop your heart, when practiced, and leave you pleasantly fulfilled and content. Healthy love relaxes your limbic system, counters the effects of fear, and assists you in the expansion of positive, uplifting abilities.

As you free love—love will free you. Developing tangible, well-practiced, alternative neural pathways of love and care will override your inherited and cultivated neural pathways of fear and selfishness, and you will begin to enjoy life like never before.

"If you can change your mind, you can change your life." — William James

Available at *Amazon.com*
and *ExploringGodsLove.com*

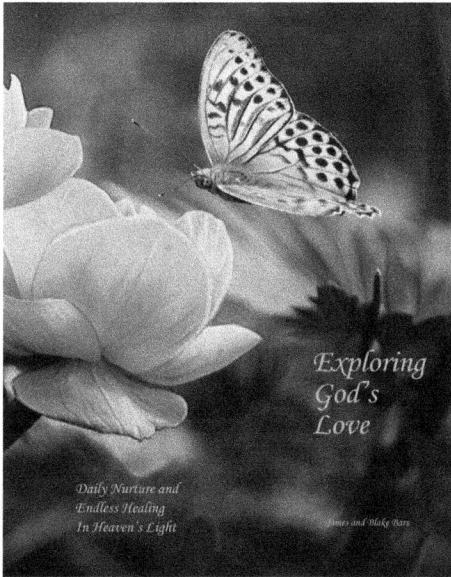

Exploring God's Love
Daily Nurture and Endless Healing in Heaven's Light

Most people desire to know safety, to belong, and to matter.
Living as an expression of God's love is the surest path to realizing your heart's desires.
It is daily nurture that enables your spirit to walk in His ways!
This engaging, love-based treatise, unites ancient light from God's word with current science to steadily nurture and heal every facet of your being.
You will know safety in Heaven's light, you will realize absolute belonging as God's beloved, and you will truly matter as an ambassador of His kingdom of love.
On your adventure, you will enjoy space to daily journal your discoveries and desires.
Your joy awaits!

This book contains much of the same material as *The Nourished Soul*. But is more focused on journaling your daily discoveries and desires.

$12.99 US and Canada

Recovery Journal
Laugh, Learn, Pray, Affirm

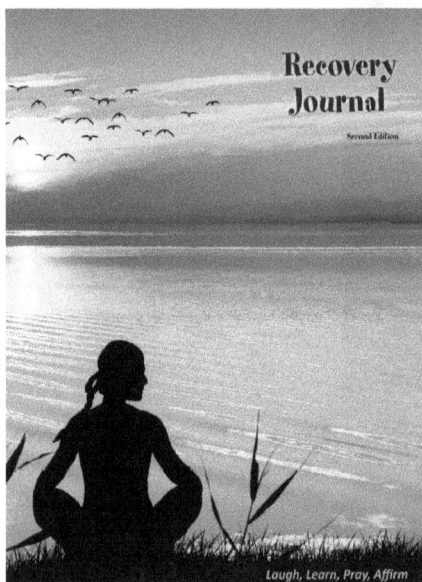

Second Edition

Journal: A personal record of intimate communion, inquiry, and reflection.
Journey: A passage from one place to another.
This book is both.
It will prove fruitful for any seeker, especially those in recovery from addiction and co-dependency.
This playful and enlightening, spiritual quest will add color to the rich horizons of your renewing mind.
You will smile and laugh.
Your meditations will enlighten the sage inside you andbrighten barricaded gardens in your soul.
Your aspiring prayers will vitalize the kingdom of God that lies within.
You will affirm your intrinsic value as heaven's child.
Your wisdom, knowledge, and understanding will strengthen.
Your hope will flourish within God's promises.
You will know the Way to your divine Father's welcoming home.

Available at *Amazon.com*
and *ExploringGod'sLove.com*

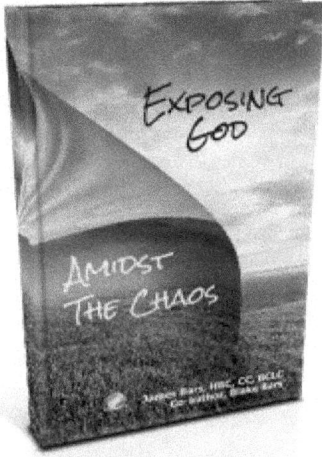

Exposing God Amidst the Chaos

Is God fair?

Is He loving?

Would a fair and loving God take His sick child and eternally torture that child for being born sick?

This is the current view of God now portrayed to the world.

Could our perception of Who He is be wrong?

Let's pull back the curtain and take a closer look at our God of love.

This is a beautiful book for souls who have been damaged by fear-based perceptions of God. It also makes a great gift for those you may wish to reach with God's message of hope.

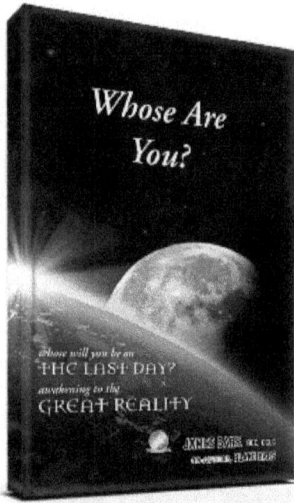

Whose Are You?

Join us as we travel back through the travail of millenniums to a galaxy far, far away. Witness the birth of darkness. Be there as our Liberator begins His counter-intuitive and radically irreligious war for universal dominion and each living souls' allegiance. Discover the Spirit, the Way and the true story behind the veil of History.

The vital messages contained within this riveting work will help enable you to walk through the valley of decision and perpetually surrender to the True Force of life.

You will know Whose You Are and be shown the Way to eternal victory as your mind and heart are awakened to the well-hidden truth of what is really happening in and around you even as you read this sentence.

There exists a deadly conspiracy, the magnitude of which is beyond unenlightened human comprehension, yet to the chosen – it has been revealed.

"Many are called but few are chosen." Matthew 22:14 NKJV

Answers are available to these crucial questions: Have I been chosen? Why am I here? Who am I? Whose am I?

Come with us and perhaps a clearer dawn will shine upon your own journey homeward.

Booklets:

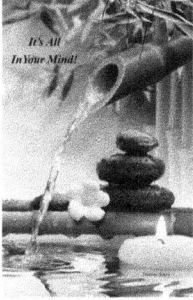

It's *All In Your Mind*
Summary of Chapter 1 of
The Nourished Soul

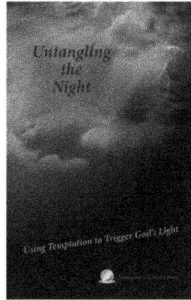

Untangling the Night
Summary of Chapter 7 of
The Nourished Soul

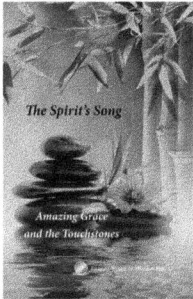

The Spirit's Song
Summary of Chapters 4 & 5 of
The Nourished Soul

IOU Love
Summary of Chapter 8 of
The Nourished Soul

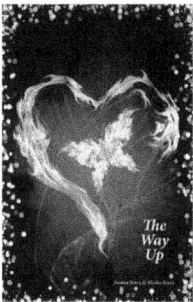

The Way Up?
Summary of Chapter 6 of
The Nourished Soul

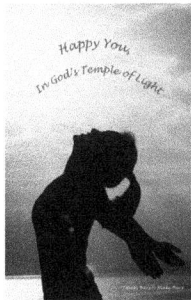

Happy You,
In God's Temple of Light
Summary of Chapter 9 of
The Nourished Soul

www.ingramcontent.com/pod-product-compliance
Lightning Source LLC
Chambersburg PA
CBHW060606030426

42337CB00019B/3632